Emotions
in the Wild

A Writer's Observation Journal

Laurel Garver

Emotions in the Wild: A Writer's
Observation Journal

Paperback edition

ISBN 978-1514197509

LWG Books
Philadelphia, Pennsylvania

Contents

Introduction

"Human life itself may be almost pure chaos, but the work of the artist is to take these handfuls of confusion and disparate things, things that seem to be irreconcilable, and put them together in a frame to give them some kind of shape and meaning." —Katherine Anne Porter

When you're writing a highly emotional scene, do you ever feel like something is missing? You have a sense of what the characters might say, but worry it sounds a bit cliché. The characters seem like talking heads, or perhaps a little wooden. Or conversely, they behave like melodramatic twits. You wish you had a better handle on how to convey their emotions not only with their speech, but also in their actions and your descriptions of them.

The best way to get a handle on real human emotion is to **observe it** "in the wild" — that is, in everyday situations you encounter while living normal life. There truly is no substitute for this kind of organic research. Simply people-watching and jotting down what you see can help you generate a great deal of helpful raw material from which to build powerfully real characters. Do this research haphazardly, however, and you could waste hours looking for vital pieces when you're deep in a draft. Organization is truly key for making observation an effective tool that strengthens your writing.

With this in mind, I have developed this book of focused journaling exercises so that you observe all kinds of real human behavior and record the information in a manner that you can easily find it again and again for use in **any** fiction project.

Unlike other writing resources that offer others' observations or research on body language, facial expressions, or emotional responses, this tool enables you to create an emotional repertoire that is uniquely yours: your personal "emotions bible." Once completed, this journal can serve as your go-to source for building emotionally-charged scenes in your own authorial voice. It will help you deepen the subtext of your scenes, ground your dialogue, and bring verisimilitude to every character exchange in every fiction project you create.

The emotions are arranged alphabetically. Each chapter opens with evocative quotes to stimulate your thinking about the essence of each emotion. After the quotes are five observation exercises: common triggers; facial signs; postures and movements; range of reactions; and finally, related words, idioms, and phrases. Each exercise is described below.

Common triggers

What events or interactions tend to trigger this emotion? Watch for genuine incidents "in the wild," rather than rely on mediated interpretations from actors in TV, film and stage plays. Actors are more likely to go for the obvious, cliché expressions and postures.

The same incident can trigger a wide range of emotional reactions: a late train will make one man frustrated, another worried, a third defeated, a fourth confused, a fifth delighted.

When you observe these varied reactions, think about what underlying desire, when met with this particular stimulus, led to this emotion. In the late train example above, the frustrated first passenger might have an underlying desire for a smooth day. The worried second passenger might want to make a good impression at an important meeting. The defeated third passenger might want a leg up on the competition at a job interview after months of unsuccessful job hunting. The confused fourth passenger might be a recent arrival to the city who wants a better sense of when the trains normally run. The delighted fifth passenger might wish to avoid a boring meeting.

Look for patterns. What stimuli seem to evoke a similar response in the most different kinds of people?

Facial signs

Observe the facial movements of people expressing this emotion. Is the brow smooth or furrowed? Do the eyebrows go up or down? Do the eyes widen or narrow? Do the nostrils flare, tighten, or remain relaxed? Does the mouth smile or frown? Are the lips relaxed, pursed, curled to one side? Do the teeth bite a lip or the inside of the cheek?

Doodle typical facial signs you see, and describe them in as much detail as you can.

Postures and movements

Emotions are conveyed not only in our faces, but also in how we carry and move our bodies. If people were masked, you could still read much of their emotion through their other body language. You don't even need to be in eavesdropping range to discern the kinds of emotions people are expressing. Their bodies shout them.

Describe in detail the postures and motions you see related to each emotion, Pay particular attention to necks, shoulders, spines, hands, arms, legs and feet. It might be helpful to draw these gestures and postures as well — even stick figures can jog your memory when it comes time to write a key scene.

If you struggle with "talking head" dialogue, this aspect of research will be especially helpful to make your writing come alive.

Range of reactions observed

How do different types of people express an emotion? Each group we belong to has its own rules about which emotions one can express freely, and which ones must be tamped down or diverted into a more acceptable expression. For example, your trash collector, grandmother, and toddler cousin will all express anger rather differently.

Try to observe a diversity of age, gender, socioeconomic, and ethnic groups. The information you gather will enable you to create a diverse range of characters to populate your stories, rather than cookie-cutter copies.

Related words, idioms, phrases

Brainstorm synonyms for this emotion, strong verbs related to it, as well as idioms (jealousy as "green-eyed monster") and phrases ("sharing is caring") associated with it. Especially be on the hunt for unique metaphors and similes that encapsulate the emotion.

Listen to the way people expressing this emotion talk about their feelings. How do they describe how they feel? What colorful expressions do you hear? Record it all.

1. Anger

"Never go to bed mad. Stay up and fight."
— Phyllis Diller

"We boil at different degrees." — Clint Eastwood

"Beware of him that is slow to anger; for when it is long coming, it is the stronger when it comes, and the longer kept. Abused patience turns to fury." — Francis Quarles

"Anger is a wind which blows out the lamp of the mind." — Robert Green Ingersoll

"Where there is anger, there is always pain underneath." — Eckhart Tolle

Common triggers

Facial signs

Postures and movements

Range of reactions observed

Related words, idioms, phrases

2. Amusement / Mirth

"Like a welcome summer rain, humor may suddenly cleanse and cool the earth, the air and you." — Langston Hughes

"Laughter is the sun that drives winter from the human face." — Victor Hugo

"The comic is the perception of the opposite; humor is the feeling of it." — Umberto Eco

"If people never did silly things nothing intelligent would ever get done." — Ludwig Wittgenstein

Common triggers

Facial signs

Postures and movements

Range of reactions observed

Related words, idioms, phrases

3. Attraction

"Everything has beauty, but not everyone sees it." — Confucius

"There is a charm about the forbidden that makes it unspeakably desirable." — Mark Twain

"Gestures, in love, are incomparably more attractive, effective and valuable than words." — François Rabelais

"I would love to say that you make me weak in the knees, but to be quite upfront and completely truthful, you make my body forget it has knees at all." — Tyler Knott Gregson

"It is amazing how complete is the delusion that beauty is goodness." — Leo Tolstoy

Common triggers

Facial signs

Postures and movements

Range of reactions observed

Related words, idioms, phrases

4. Awe / Reverence

"Dwell on the beauty of life. Watch the stars, and see yourself running with them." — Marcus Aurelius

"Gratitude bestows reverence, allowing us to encounter everyday epiphanies, those transcendent moments of awe that change forever how we experience life and the world." — John Milton

"He who can no longer pause to wonder and stand rapt in awe, is as good as dead; his eyes are closed." — Albert Einstein

Common triggers

Facial signs

Postures and movements

Range of reactions observed

Related words, idioms, phrases

5. Bliss / Euphoria

"...completely, and perfectly, and incandescently happy." — Jane Austen

"To burn always with this hard, gem-like flame, to maintain this ecstasy, is success in life." — Walter Pater

"That is happiness — to be dissolved into something complete and great." — Willa Cather

"Some place the bliss in action, some in ease, Those call it pleasure, and contentment these." — Alexander Pope

Common triggers

Facial signs

Postures and movements

Range of reactions observed

Related words, idioms, phrases

6. Boredom

"Boredom is an emptiness filled with insistence."
— Leo Stein

"All man's troubles come from not knowing how to sit still in one room." — Blaise Pascal

"Boredom is the conviction that you can't change...the shriek of unused capacities."
— Saul Bellow

"There are no uninteresting things, only uninterested people." — G.K. Chesterton

Common triggers

Facial signs

Postures and movements

Range of reactions observed

Related words, idioms, phrases

7. Compassion / Caring

"You care so much you feel as though you will bleed to death with the pain of it." — J.K. Rowling

"When will our consciences grow so tender that we will act to prevent human misery rather than avenge it?" — Eleanor Roosevelt

"Caring is not a finite resource…it's like a muscle: the more you exercise it, the stronger it gets." — Jonathan Safran Foer

"Let us touch the dying, the poor, the lonely and the unwanted according to the graces we have received and let us not be ashamed or slow to do the humble work." — Mother Teresa

Common triggers

Facial signs

Postures and movements

Range of reactions observed

Related words, idioms, phrases

8. Confusion

"I had nothing to offer anybody except my own confusion." — Jack Kerouac

"A bitter and perplexed 'What shall I do?' is worse to man than worst necessity." — Samuel Taylor Coleridge

"I can't say as ever I was lost, but I was bewildered once for three days." — Daniel Boone

"I pretty much try to stay in a constant state of confusion just because of the expression it leaves on my face." — Dana Carvey

Common triggers

Facial signs

Postures and movements

Range of reactions observed

Related words, idioms, phrases

9. Courage

"Boldness is a mask for fear, however great."
— John Dryden

"We cannot banish dangers, but we can banish fears. We must not demean life by standing in awe of death." — David Sarnoff

"…we often can't see the ways in which we are being strong — like, you can't be aware of what you're doing that's tough and brave at the time that you're doing it because if you knew that it was brave, then you'd be scared." — Lena Dunham

"In order to achieve anything, you must be brave enough to fail." — Kirk Douglas

Common triggers

Facial signs

Postures and movements

Range of reactions observed

Related words, idioms, phrases

10. Curiosity

"The cure for boredom is curiosity. There is no cure for curiosity." — Dorothy Parker

"There are no foolish questions, and no man becomes a fool until he has stopped asking questions." — Charles Proteus Steinmetz

"The possession of knowledge does not kill the sense of wonder and mystery. There is always more mystery." — Anaïs Nin

"I keep six honest serving-men,
They taught me all I knew;
Their names are What and Why and When
And How and Where and Who."
— Rudyard Kipling

Common triggers

Facial signs

Postures and movements

Range of reactions observed

Related words, idioms, phrases

11. Defeat / Discouragement

"My life has become a dismal sigh fettered
by pangs of grief and anguished weeping."
— Richelle E. Goodrich

"Life is truly known only to those who suffer,
lose, endure adversity and stumble from defeat
to defeat." — Anaïs Nin

"Sometimes I feel my whole life has been one big
rejection." — Marilyn Monroe

"Death is nothing, but to live defeated and
inglorious is to die daily." — Napoleon Bonaparte

Common triggers

Facial signs

Postures and movements

Range of reactions observed

Related words, idioms, phrases

12. Desire / Longing

"Love is often gentle, desire always a rage."
— Mignon McLaughlin

"Chase down your passion like it's the last bus of the night." — Terri Guillemets

"Desire, like the atom, is explosive with creative force." — Paul Vernon Buser

"We are homesick most for the places we have never known." — Carson McCullers

"I didn't know then what I wanted, but the ache for it was palpable." — Sue Monk Kidd

Common triggers

Facial signs

Postures and movements

Range of reactions observed

Related words, idioms, phrases

13. Determination

"Victory is always possible for the person who refuses to stop fighting." — Napoleon Hill

"I ask not for a lighter burden, but for broader shoulders." — Jewish Proverb

"Every moment of resistance to temptation is a victory." — Frederick William Faber

"The rewards for those who persevere far exceed the pain that must precede the victory." — Ted Engstrom

Common triggers

Facial signs

Postures and movements

Range of reactions observed

Related words, idioms, phrases

14. Disgust

"All is disgust when a man leaves his own nature and does what is unfit." — Sophocles

"The color is repellant, almost revolting: a smouldering unclean yellow...." — Charlotte Perkins Gilman

"All this class of pleasures inspires me with the same nausea I feel at the sight of rich plum-cake...." — Sydney Smith

"A surging, seething, murmuring crowd of beings that are human only in name, for to the eye and ear they seem naught but savage creatures, animated by vile passions...." — Emma Orczy

"A voice can also repel, infuriate or actually make a listener ill." — Johnny Olson

Common triggers

Facial signs

Postures and movements

Range of reactions observed

Related words, idioms, phrases

15. Dreaminess

"The reason I talk to myself is because I'm the only one whose answers I accept." — George Carlin

"For my part I know nothing with any certainty, but the sight of the stars makes me dream." — Vincent Van Gogh

"Cherish your visions and your dreams as they are the children of your soul, the blueprints of your ultimate achievements." — Napoleon Hill

"Without leaps of imagination, or dreaming, we lose the excitement of possibilities. Dreaming, after all, is a form of planning." — Gloria Steinem

Common triggers

Facial signs

Postures and movements

Range of reactions observed

Related words, idioms, phrases

16. Embarrassment / Humiliation

"We're often afraid of looking at our shadow because we want to avoid the shame or embarrassment that comes along with admitting mistakes." — Marianne Williamson

"If someone tells you often enough you're worthless, you start to believe it." — Kierston Wareing

"What makes the pain we feel from shame and jealousy so cutting is that vanity can give us no assistance in bearing them." — François de La Rochefoucauld

"Blushing is the most peculiar and most human of all expressions." — Charles Darwin

Common triggers

Facial signs

Postures and movements

Range of reactions observed

Related words, idioms, phrases

17. Envy

"Envy is the art of counting the other fellow's blessings instead of your own." — Harold Coffin

"Our envy always lasts longer than the happiness of those we envy." — François de La Rochefoucauld

"Envy is a symptom of lack of appreciation of our own uniqueness and self worth."
— Elizabeth O'Connor

"The grass is always greener on the other side of the fence." — Proverb

Common triggers

Facial signs

Postures and movements

Range of reactions observed

Related words, idioms, phrases

18. Excitement / Anticipation

"Looking forward to things is half the pleasure of them." — Lucy Maud Montgomery

"...anticipation of happiness can sometimes be as gratifying as its consummation." — Gaynor Arnold

"It is always with excitement that I wake up in the morning wondering what my intuition will toss up to me, like gifts from the sea." — Jonas Salk

"I sat down and tried to rest. I could not; though I had been on foot all day, I could not now repose an instant; I was too much excited. A phase of my life was closing tonight, a new one opening tomorrow: impossible to slumber in the interval; I must watch feverishly while the change was being accomplished." — Charlotte Brontë

Common triggers

Facial signs

Postures and movements

Range of reactions observed

Related words, idioms, phrases

19. Fatigue

"I feel all thin, sort of stretched, if you know what I mean: like butter that has been scraped over too much bread." — J.R.R. Tolkien

"I am sick and tired of being sick and tired." —Fannie Lou Hamer

"Although she was giddy with exhaustion, sleep was a lover who refused to be touched...." — Janet Fitch

"I felt her weariness then, and with it, my own. I felt it dark and heavy upon me, darker and heavier than any drug they ever gave me — it seemed heavy as death." — Sarah Waters

Common triggers

Facial signs

Postures and movements

Range of reactions observed

Related words, idioms, phrases

20. Fear

"She had a strange feeling in the pit of her stomach, like when you're swimming and you want to put your feet down on something solid, but the water's deeper than you think and there's nothing there." — Julia Gregson

"Stare at the dark too long and you will eventually see what isn't there." — Cameron Jace

"I wasn't afraid of anything until I had a kid. Then I was terrified because immediately I could imagine a hundred ways in which I could not protect him." — John Irving

Common triggers

Facial signs

Postures and movements

Range of reactions observed

Related words, idioms, phrases

21. Frustration / Annoyance

"We are irritated by rascals, intolerant of fools, and prepared to love the rest. But where are they?" — Mignon McLaughlin

"Family love is messy, clinging, and of an annoying and repetitive pattern, like bad wallpaper." — P.J. O'Rourke

"Our faults irritate us most when we see them in others." — Proverb

"Some people deserve a high five
In the face
With a chair." — Author unknown

Common triggers

Facial signs

Postures and movements

Range of reactions observed

Related words, idioms, phrases

22. Gratitude

"Gratitude changes the pangs of memory into a tranquil joy." — Dietrich Bonhoeffer

"Some people are always grumbling because roses have thorns; I am thankful that thorns have roses." — Alphonse Karr

"Appreciation is the highest form of prayer, for it acknowledges the presence of good wherever you shine the light of your thankful thoughts." — Alan Cohen

"Gratitude bestows reverence, allowing us to encounter everyday epiphanies, those transcendent moments of awe that change forever how we experience life and the world." — John Milton

"...gratitude is happiness doubled by wonder." — G.K. Chesterton

Common triggers

Facial signs

Postures and movements

Range of reactions observed

Related words, idioms, phrases

23. Guilt / Remorse

"Guilt has very quick ears to an accusation."
— Henry Fielding

"There is no refuge from memory and remorse in this world. The spirits of our foolish deeds haunt us, with or without repentance." — Gilbert Parker

"Suspicion always haunts the guilty mind."
— William Shakespeare

"There is no person so severely punished, as those who subject themselves to the whip of their own remorse." — Lucius Annaeus Seneca

Common triggers

Facial signs

Postures and movements

Range of reactions observed

Related words, idioms, phrases

24. Happiness

"The secret of happiness is not in doing what one likes, but in liking what one does." — James M. Barrie

"There are souls in this world who have the gift of finding joy everywhere and leaving it behind them when they go." — Frederick William Faber

"Happiness consists of living each day as if it were the first day of your honeymoon and the last day of your vacation." — Leo Tolstoy

"When you finally allow yourself to trust joy and embrace it, you will find you dance with everything." — Ralph Waldo Emerson

Common triggers

Facial signs

Postures and movements

Range of reactions observed

Related words, idioms, phrases

25. Hate / Resentment

"From the deepest desires often come the deadliest hate." — Socrates

"Resentment is like drinking poison and waiting for the other person to die." — Malachy McCourt

"It is remarkable by how much a pinch of malice enhances the penetrating power of an idea or an opinion. Our ears, it seems, are wonderfully attuned to sneers and evil reports about our fellow men." — Eric Hoffer

"Malice can always find a mark to shoot at, and a pretense to fire." — Charles Simmons

Common triggers

Facial signs

Postures and movements

Range of reactions observed

Related words, idioms, phrases

26. Hope

"'Hope' is the thing with feathers—
That perches in the soul—
And sings the tune without the words—
And never stops — at all...."
— Emily Dickinson

"Hope begins in the dark, the stubborn hope that if you just show up and try to do the right thing, the dawn will come." — Anne Lamott

"Hope is putting faith to work when doubting would be easier." — Thomas S. Monson

"Hope is the only bee that makes honey without flowers." — Robert Ingersoll

Common triggers

Facial signs

Postures and movements

Range of reactions observed

Related words, idioms, phrases

27. Hurt

"Life is made up of sobs, sniffles, and smiles, with sniffles predominating." — O. Henry

"That's the funny thing about old hurts — they just wait for new heartache to come along and then show up, just as sharp and horrible as the first day you woke up with the world changed all around you." — Lilith Saintcrow

"When I got heartbroken at 20, it just felt like someone had spiraled a football right into my skull. At 40, it feels like someone had driven a 757 right through me." — Junot Diaz

"Pain insists upon being attended to. God whispers to us in our pleasures, speaks in our consciences, but shouts in our pains. It is his megaphone to rouse a deaf world." — C.S. Lewis

Common triggers

Facial signs

Postures and movements

Range of reactions observed

Related words, idioms, phrases

28. Indignation

"Injustice is outrageous and deserves outrage."
— Chris Hayes

"...to be angry with the right person and to the right degree and at the right time and for the right purpose, and in the right way — that is not within everybody's power and is not easy." — Aristotle

"The world often continues to allow evil because it isn't angry enough." — Bede Jarrett

"What really raises one's indignation against suffering is not suffering intrinsically, but the senselessness of suffering." — Friedrich Nietzsche

Common triggers

Facial signs

Postures and movements

Range of reactions observed

Related words, idioms, phrases

29. Jealousy

"Handsome husbands often make a wife's heart ache." — Samuel Richardson

"Jealousy injures us with the dagger of self-doubt." — Terri Guillemets

"Your sweetheart calls you by another's name. His eyes linger too long on your best friend. He talks with excitement about a girl at work. And the fire catches. Jealousy — that sickening combination of possessiveness, suspicion, rage, and humiliation — can overtake your mind and threaten your very core as you contemplate your rival." — Helen Fisher

"Jealousy is the great exaggerator." — Johann Christoph Friedrich von Schiller

Common triggers

Facial signs

Postures and movements

Range of reactions observed

Related words, idioms, phrases

30. Loneliness

"Everyone at some point in their lives feels excluded and misunderstood." — Hugh Bonneville

"The most terrible poverty is loneliness, and the feeling of being unloved." — Mother Teresa

"Who knows what true loneliness is — not the conventional word but the naked terror? To the lonely themselves it wears a mask. The most miserable outcast hugs some memory or some illusion." — Joseph Conrad

"A lonely man is a lonesome thing, a stone, a bone, a stick, a receptacle for Gilbey's gin, a stooped figure sitting at the edge of a hotel bed, heaving copious sighs like the autumn wind." — John Cheever

Common triggers

Facial signs

Postures and movements

Range of reactions observed

Related words, idioms, phrases

31. Love

"Since love grows within you, so beauty grows. For love is the beauty of the soul." — St. Augustine

"Love is but the discovery of ourselves in others, and the delight in the recognition." — Alexander Smith

"The best love is the kind that awakens the soul; that makes us reach for more, that plants the fire in our hearts and brings peace to our minds." — Nicholas Sparks

"At the touch of love everyone becomes a poet." — Plato

"You know it's love when all you want is that person to be happy, even if you're not part of their happiness." — Julia Roberts

Common triggers

Facial signs

Postures and movements

Range of reactions observed

Related words, idioms, phrases

32. Nervousness

"My nerves needed a break, not a reminder of how much trouble we were in. I prowled around, but it didn't help. I still felt like my skin was on too tight." — Karen Chance

"Oh the nerves, the nerves; the mysteries of this machine called man! Oh the little that unhinges it, poor creatures that we are!" — Charles Dickens

"I always felt caged, closed in, like I was punching at things that weren't there. I always had too much energy for the room I was in." — Angelina Jolie

Common triggers

Facial signs

Postures and movements

Range of reactions observed

Related words, idioms, phrases

33. Pride

"Accept the challenges so that you can feel the exhilaration of victory." — George S. Patton

"Today's accomplishments were yesterday's impossibilities." — Robert H. Schuller

"Happiness does not come from doing easy work but from the afterglow of satisfaction that comes after the achievement of a difficult task that demanded our best." — Theodore Rubin

"I look back on my life like a good day's work, it was done and I am satisfied with it." — Grandma Moses

Common triggers

Facial signs

Postures and movements

Range of reactions observed

Related words, idioms, phrases

34. Sadness / Grief

"Give sorrow words; the grief that does not speak whispers the o'er-fraught heart and bids it break." — William Shakespeare

"Where you used to be, there is a hole in the world, which I find myself constantly walking around in the daytime, and falling in at night." — Edna St. Vincent Millay

"Deep grief sometimes is almost like a specific location, a coordinate on a map of time. When you are standing in that forest of sorrow, you cannot imagine that you could ever find your way to a better place." — Elizabeth Gilbert

Common triggers

Facial signs

Postures and movements

Range of reactions observed

Related words, idioms, phrases

35. Shock

"There is only one kind of shock worse than the totally unexpected: the expected for which one has refused to prepare." — Mary Renault

"Life is unfair, unkind and unforeseeable. It knocks you down when you least expect it."
— Lisa De Jong

"There is a feeling of disbelief that comes over you, that takes over, and you kind of go through the motions. You do what you're supposed to do, but in fact you're not there at all." — Frederick Barthelme

Common triggers

Facial signs

Postures and movements

Range of reactions observed

Related words, idioms, phrases

36. Surprise / Delight

"The moments of happiness we enjoy take us by surprise. It is not that we seize them, but that they seize us." — Ashley Montagu

"Think of your favorite teacher you ever had in school: the one who made it the most fun to go to class. They surprise you. They keep you guessing. They keep you coming back, wanting to know what's going to happen next." — Pete Carroll

The true delight is in the finding out rather than in the knowing. — Isaac Asimov

"There is no such thing as the pursuit of happiness, but there is the discovery of joy." — Joyce Grenfell

Common triggers

Facial signs

Postures and movements

Range of reactions observed

Related words, idioms, phrases

37. Tranquility / Peace

"The pursuit, even of the best things, ought to be calm and tranquil." — Cicero

"I want the soft-pillow feeling that I associate with memories of being ill when I was younger, soft pillows and fresh linens and satin-edged blankets and hot chocolate. It's not so much the comfort itself as knowing there's someone who wants to take care of you." — Franny Billingsley

"A true friend encourages us, comforts us, supports us like a big easy chair, offering us a safe refuge from the world." — H. Jackson Brown, Jr.

"They have most satisfaction in themselves, and consequently the sweetest relish of their creature comforts." — Matthew Henry

Common triggers

Facial signs

Postures and movements

Range of reactions observed

Related words, idioms, phrases

38. Wariness / Caution

"Better a thousand times careful than once dead." — Proverb

"Don't ever take a fence down until you know why it was put up." — Robert Frost

"Men walk this tightrope where any sign of weakness illicits shame, and so they're afraid to make themselves vulnerable for fear of looking weak." — Brene Brown

"Carelessness doesn't bounce; it shatters."
— Terri Guillemets

Common triggers

Facial signs

Postures and movements

Range of reactions observed

Related words, idioms, phrases

39. Worry / Anxiety

"As a rule, what is out of sight disturbs men's minds more seriously than what they see."
— Julius Caesar

"Man is not worried by real problems so much as by his imagined anxieties about real problems." — Epictetus

"Worry is like a rocking chair: It gives you something to do, but never gets you anywhere."
— Erma Bombeck

"But I can hardly sit still. I keep fidgeting, crossing one leg and then the other. I feel like I could throw off sparks, or break a window — maybe rearrange all the furniture." — Raymond Carver

Common triggers

Facial signs

Postures and movements

Range of reactions observed

Related words, idioms, phrases

Acknowledgements

Special thanks to Prof. E. Ross Genzel, whose theater class Basic Movement inspired me to journal observations about motion and emotion.

Thanks to my beta readers, Connor Bartholomew and Beth Frear, for their insightful feedback and encouragement.

Thanks to my husband and daughter for keeping me engaged in the real world when I'd rather cloister myself with imaginary people and their dilemmas.

Also by Laurel Garver

Writing When You Can't Write*:*
Tips and tools to develop your fiction when life drags you from the keyboard

What happens to your fiction projects when you just can't write? Maybe a major project is due at your day job, a family member is in crisis, or you've been hit hard with an illness. Chances are, you abruptly drop your writing project and focus on the crisis *du jour*. And when you return to your writing, it can take weeks to get back on track — weeks of deep doubt and fear.

Fear no longer. This guide offers a myriad of exercises, techniques, and tools to develop and stay connected with any fiction project, no matter how chaotic life becomes.

Coming Fall 2015

Never Gone, fiction

Teen artist Dani Deane feels like the universe
has imploded when her father dies. Days after
his death, she sees him leafing through sketches
in her room, roaming the halls at church,
wandering his own wake. Is grief making her
crazy? Or is her dad truly adrift between this
world and the next, trying to contact her?

Dani longs for his help as she tries and fails to
connect with her workaholic mother. Her pain
only deepens when astonishing secrets about
her family history come to light. But Dani finds a
surprising ally in Theo, the quiet guy lingering in
the backstage of her life. He persistently reaches
out as Dani's faith falters, her family relation-
ships unravel, and she withdraws into a
dangerous obsession with her father's ghostly
appearances. Will she let her broken, prodigal
heart find reason to hope again?

Muddy-fingered Midnights, poems

An eclectic mix of light and dark, playful and
spiritual, lyric and narrative free verse. In an
intricate dance of sound play, it explores how
our perceptions shape our interactions with the
world. Here child heroes emerge on playgrounds
and in chicken coops, teens grapple with grief
and taste first love, adults waver between
isolation and engaged connection. It is a book
about creative life, our capacity to wound and
heal, and the unlikely places we find love,
beauty, and grace.

22171947R00122

Printed in Great Britain
by Amazon